A. LECONTE PUBLISHERS
8, 10, Avenue Henri-Barbusse
94200 IVRY-SUR-SEINE

FROM LUTETIA TO THE PRESENT DAY

This picture book of Paris is not intended as a guide. And while it does not hold you to any itineraries, we have divided it up into a number of pleasant walks for you to enjoy at your leisure. Each of these walks begins at Notre-Dame, the privileged site at the heart of the Ile de la Cité whence all the roads of France begin.

Initially a small hamlet of fishermen from the tribe of the Parisii who settled on the largest island of the River Seine, the town of Lutetia, insurgent against Caesar (52 BC), was attacked by Labienus, who sailed down the Seine to site of Saint-Germain l'Auxerrois on the Right Bank. The Gaul chief Camulogène was camped on the Left Bank on the location of Saint-Germain-des-Prés. With the aid of a stratagem, victory went to the Roman legions.

Under the rule of the first emperors, Lutetia was a pleasant province town. To its deities the Ile de la Cité dedicated its temples, to the ruling powers an imperial palace. Initially the town grew on the Left Bank, along the road to Orléans. Under Tiberius, a new town began to cover the hill later to become St Geneviève. The Luxembourg Gardens correspond to the centre of that prosperous quarter. The arenas were located on the other side of the hill, extra muros.

From 258 onwards, Lutetia was gradually destroyed by the barbarian invasions. The inhabitants of the town sought refuge on the Ile de la Cité, hastily fortified. At the end of a new invasion, in 355, the Emperor Constance despatched his brother-in-law, Julian the Apostate, as governor of northern Gaul. He settled in Lutetia, in the Cité, where he was proclaimed Emperor by his legionaries in 360. One century later, the Huns arrived at the gates of Lutetia. St.Geneviève rallied the population not to flee, and saved the Cité.

The Merovingian kings built a capital but the palaces, the wooden walls put up by these Franks, disappeared along with the dynasty. The Carolingian kings chose to move their capitals further to the east of the Empire. In 855 Lutetia, now named Paris and still in the Cité, blocked the Seine to Danes out to sack the towns further upstream. The defences were under the command of Eudes, Count of France. The Danes are repelled, and the count receives the elected title of king to become the first Capetian. It is the start of the good fortunes of Paris, which subsequently developed on both banks, around the monasteries.

In 1183 Philippe-Auguste orders the construction of two market halls for the town's merchants; in 1186 the town is paved; 1190 sees the building of the rampart of the Right Bank; in 1209, the Left Bank enclosure goes up. It is a period of construction both inside and outside the walls. The king protects his ramparts, on the Seine, with the massive keep of the Louvre...

Charles V (1364-1388) builds a second fortified wall, on the Right Bank, enclosing the Hôtel St-Paul, the king's new residence; the Célestins; the Maison du Temple; Saint-Martin-des-Champs; Saint-Nicholas-des-Champs; Rue Montorgueil; Rue Montmartre. The wall eventually joins up with the Seine and the Louvre, its course more or less that of the Rue d'Aboukir, the Place des Victoires, the Palais-Royal. The wall is fortified particularly to the east by "La Bastille", a mighty fortress, guarding the road to Vincennes.

In the 16th century and at the beginning of the 17th century, the town continues to expand to the west, so much so that Louis XIII extends the Paris of Charles V by a wall which surrounds it, from the Porte Saint-Denis to the limits of the Tuileries.

The young Louis XIV, marked by the humiliation of the Fronde uprising, set up his government in Versailles. He nevertheless improved the appearance of his capital, transformed the Louvre, erected the Hôtel des Invalides, La Salpêtrière and the Observatory, encircling the town with a ring of triumphal gates, creating the Place des Victoires et Place Vendôme...

It is to Louis XV that we owe the Concorde, the Ecole Militaire (military academy), the Hôtel de la Monnaie, the Palais de Justice (law courts). Under the reign of Louis XVI, however, the face of Paris was to change radically as a result of three essential measures: The width regulation for all new streets, set at 9.75 m (around 30 ft) wide; the building in 1784 of the Fermiers Généraux wall, which carried the outskirts of Paris to the outside boulevards; the destruction of all the houses built on the bridges of Paris. Suddenly, long uninterrupted views of the Seine, as we known them today, were opened up for the first time.

Napoleon I vowed to make Paris the "most beautiful city ever to exist". In his mind, there could be no architecture without town planning: he went on to create bridges, quays, market halls, slaughter houses, the Arc de Triomphe at the Etoile, the large thoroughfares, churches, but also water distribution: under his reign, the waters of the Ourcq are channelled to Paris, bassin de la Villette, aqueducts and countless public fountains.

The Restoration was marked in particular by the creation of a new quarter, the aristocratic Faubourg Saint-Germain.

The last major changes before the Paris of the 20th century occurred under Napoleon III, with the substantial works of Baron Haussmann, together with the random industrialization of the suburbs and outskirts. Next came the universal exhibition of 1889 and the building of what initially was the most controversial and later the most famous monument, the Eiffel Tower... And even today, Paris has by no means come to rest...

All around Paris, the royal and baronial halls of the Ile de France, located only a few miles from the city, served as country houses, places of refuge, sometimes even as substitute capitals, permanent ones such as Versailles or seasonal ones such as Fontainebleau... We shall visit some of them, at the end of this book.

The Arenas of Lutetia, a monument of Gallo-Roman times, were destroyed by the great invasions of 280, buried, and finally brought to light during construction work on the Rue Monge in 1869. They were uncovered and restored around 1900. They are thought to have been built under Tiberius. In the background the Tour Jussieu, the observatory of the Academy of Sciences.

The Beaubourg Quarter.

The George Pompidou National Art and Culture Centre (R.Piano and R.Rogers, architects).

Libraries - Exhibition and documentation halls.

FROM NOTRE-DAME TO THE OPERA

Let's set off from the heart of the Cité to discover the Right Bank of the Seine: the Tour Saint-Jacques-la-Boucherie, the Place du Châtelet, and the Palais Royal take us to the Louvre from where we will rejoin the sweeping perspectives of the Concorde, Etoile and Champs-Elysées. We will follow them to the Concorde to reach the Madeleine by the Rue Royale and finish with the Opera Quarter.

View from the south tower of Notre-Dame, the spire, the Seine upstream with the Pont de la Tournelle and the Pont de Sully, to the left, the Ile Saint-Louis.

View of the Seine, taken from one of the towers of the Church of Saint-Gervais. In the foreground the rooftops of the Hôtel-de-Ville, then the Pont Notre-Dame, the Pont au Change, to the left, the Conciergerie and the Palais, further on the Pont-Neuf, the Pont des Arts, the Pont du Carrousel, the Pont-Royal.
▼

The Cathedral of Notre-Dame: the western façade started in 1204; the towers and galleries were completed in 1250. While the central portal features the theme of the Last Judgement, the south and north portals are dedicated to the Virgin; the south portal relates her lifestory, the north portal her glorification.
▶

From the gallery of Notre-Dame, where fabulous gargoyles perch, to the north: the Tour St-Jacques and the hill of Montmartre dominated by the Sacré-Coeur.

Aerial view of Notre-Dame and its north side. ▼

The bell-tower of the Church of Saint-Jacques-la-Boucherie, the remains of the church of the butchers' guild set up near the Grand Châtelet. The Church was demolished in 1803 and only the bell-tower remains (16th century).

Place du Châtelet: the Victory Fountain, also known as the palm-tree fountain, commemorates the victories of Napoleon I, the Tour Saint-Jacques.

▲
To the right, Saint-Germain l'Auxerrois. Its architecture bears witness to the continual modifications it underwent between the 18th and 19th centuries.
To the left, the belfry, built in 1860, and the town hall of the First Arrondissement (1859).

The gardens of the Palais Royal, surrounded by buildings by the architect Victor Louis, from 1781 to 1784, commissioned by Louis-Philippe d'Orléans, the Regent's great-great-grandchild, who turned the Palais Royal into a commercial enterprise, with apartment houses, shops and various attractions. ▶

The Cour d'Honneur (Courtyard of Honour) of the Palais Royal, (18th and 19th centuries), recently embellished by the columns of the sculptor Buren. (The Palais itself, built under Richelieu, bequeathed to Louis XIV, was presented to the Duke of Orléans).
▼

The pyramid of the new Louvre, a work by the architect Pei (1988). ▶

▲ The Arc de Triomphe du Carrousel, begun in 1806, completed in 1808, modelled by Percier and Fontaine of the Arch of the Roman emperor Septimum Severus, commemorates the victories of Napoleon I during his campaign of 1805. In its axis, the obelisk of the Concorde and the Arc de l'Etoile.

The palace and gardens of the Louvre, the south façade and the south-west corner of the Napoleon III wing. ▼

THE LOUVRE

Charles V ordered that the Louvre castle built by Philippe Auguste in 1200 be virtually entirely reconstructed. But the king's residence was at the Hôtel de Saint-Paul; Charles VI also resided there. Charles VII, Dauphin and later king, and his successors, withdrew to the Loire valley.

François I ordered new construction work. Pierre Lescot, who died in 1571, was to build, under Henri II, Charles IX and Henri III, the west and south wings of the square courtyard, together with Jean Goujon.

Catherine de Médicis, however, ordered the construction, by Philibert Delorme and later by Bullant, of the Tuileries, opposite the Louvre, 500 yards further downstream. The Galerie du Bord-de-l'Eau (Water's Edge Gallery) links up the two palaces and is completed under Henri IV, who added another level.

Louis XIII and later Louis XIV extended the surface area of the buildings of the old Louvre by more than four times, with architects such as Le Mercier, Le Vau, Le Brun, Cl. Perrault. In 1662, the household left for Versailles and work is abandoned at the planning stage.

The square courtyard is completed under Napoleon by Percier and Fontaine, and work begins on the great north gallery, which is subsequently completed under Napoleon III by Visconti and then Lefuel. The insurgent Commune in 1871 set fire to the Tuileries. Finally, the Third Republic orders the reconstruction by Lefuel of the symmetrical pavilions of Marsan and Flore.

First a royal castle, later an imperial palace, the Louvre has remained the museum it was initially, with the collections of François I. Today, with its more than 250 exhibition rooms, it ranks among the world's leading museums.

The Arc de Triomphe du Carrousel floodlit.

The Marsan Pavilion, seen from the gardens.

Egyptian art (ca. 2500 BC - 5th Dynasty)
"The Seated Scribe"

Andrea Mantegna (Isola di Carturo, Padua,
1431 - Mantua 1506): "St Sebastian"
(detail).

Greek Hellenistic art (end of the 3rd century
to 1st century BC)

"The Venus de Milo".

The School of Rhodes (ca. 190 BC):
"Winged Victory of Samothrace" ▶

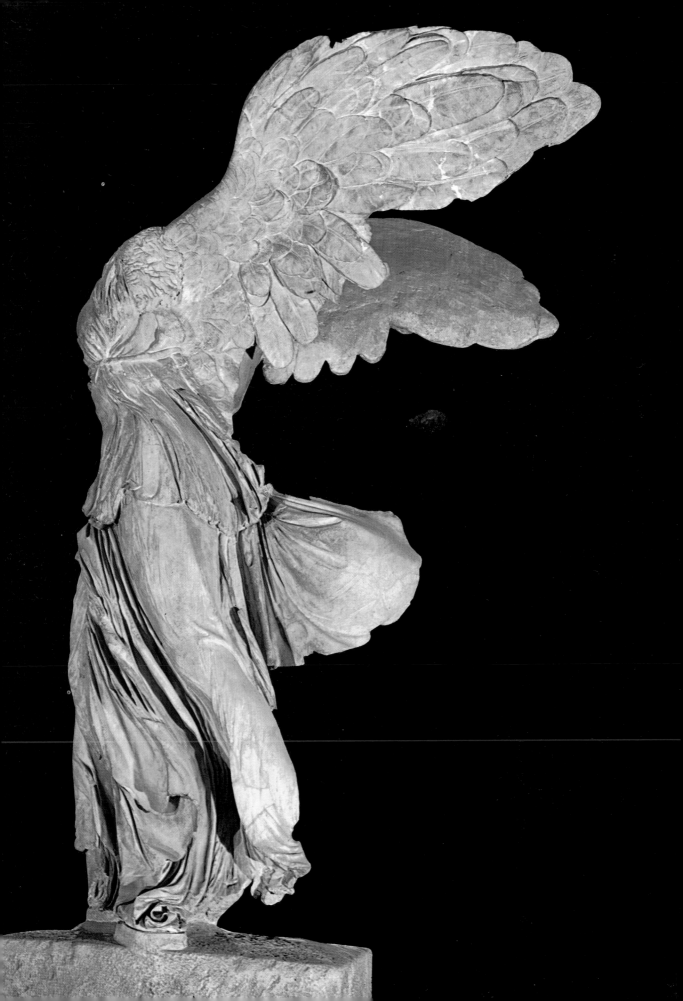

Leonardo da Vinci (Vinci 1452 - Le Clos Lucé 1519): The "Mona Lisa"

Raphael (Raffaello Santi or Sanzio - Urbino 1483 - Rome 1520): "Portrait of Joan of Aragon".

Michelangelo (Buonarroti - Caprese 1475 - Rome 1564): The Slave.

El Greco (Domenicos Théotocopoulos, named El Greco - Crete 1541 - Toledo 1614): Christ on the cross, adorated by the doners.

Peter Paul Rubens (Sigen 1577 - Anvers 1640): "Maria of Medicis": The capture of the village of Juliers.

Tintoretto (Jacopo Robusti, named Tintoretto: Venice 1518-1594): "Susanna bathing"

Jean-Antoine Watteau (Valenciennes 1684 - Nogent-sur-Marne 1721): "Gilles".

Titian (Tiziano Vecellio - Pieve di Cadore 1477? - Venice 1576): "Portrait of Françoisl".

17

José Ribera (named El Españoleto - Valencia 1589 - Napoli 1652): "Le club foot"

Murillo (Bartolomé Esteban Murillo - Sevilla 1618-1682): "The young beggar".

Camille Corot (Paris 1796, Ville d'Avray 1875): "Chartres Cathedral".
◄

►

Marie Louise Elisabeth Vigée le Brun (Paris 1755-1842): "Portrait of the artist and his daughter".

Georges De La Tour (Vic sur Seille 1593 - Lunéville 1652): "The Adoration of the Shepherds".

Nicolas Poussin (Villers 1594 - Rome 1665): "The rape of the Sabine women".

Claude Lorrain (Claude Gelée, named Lorrain - Chamagne, 1600 - Rome 1682): "View of a sea port".

Francisco De Goya y Lucientes (Fuentedetodos 1746 - Bordeaux 1828): "Doña Rita de Barrenechea".

Aristide Maillol (1861-1944), bronze, in the gardens of the Louvre.

Jean-François Millet (Gruchy 1814 - Barbizon 1875): "The Gleaners".

Antoine-Jean Gros (Paris 1771-1835): "General Bonaparte at the bridge of Arcole".

The arcades of the Rue de Rivoli, opened by Napoleon I.

Place des Pyramides - Joan of Arc, by Fremiet.

The Musée d'Orsay (Orsay Museum): Museum of 19th century art inaugurated in 1987 in the renovated surroundings of the former Orléans railway station.

Opposite, the Place de la Concorde with the pink granite Obelisk from the Temple of Luxor.
▶

The Place de la Concorde, designed by Gabriel for Louis XV.

The Champs-Elysées roundabout, a crossroads draughted by Le Nôtre in 1667.

Statue of Clemenceau, the "Father of Victory", by F. Cogné (1932).

The Grand Palais

The Petit Palais and the Grand Palais were built for the universal exhibition of 1900. The Petit Palais houses the Museum of Fine Arts of the City of Paris (Beaux-Arts). The Grand Palais, a cultural centre, is the venue for major art exhibitions.

The Petit Palais

Construction work on the Avenue des Champs-Elysées, a promenade designed by Le Nôtre in 1667, in open countryside, began under the Restoration and during the Second Empire in particular.

Top: view from the Place de la Concorde to the Arc de Triomphe; in the foreground, the Horses of Marly, a work by Coustou.

Bottom: view from the Arc de Triomphe to the Concorde. Right: the floodlighting on 14th July, the national holiday.

(Inset: the sign of the famous Lido music hall.)

AV. FOCH

AV. V. HUGO

AV. KLEBER

AV. D'IENA

AV. MARCEAU

CHAMPS ELYSEES

AV. DE FRIEDLAND

AV. DE LA Gde ARMÉE

AV. CARNOT

AV. MAC MAHON

AV. DE WAGRAM

AV. HOCHE

The Arc de Triomphe de l'Etoile, commissioned by Napoleon in 1806, from the architect Jean Chalgrin, in honour of the Grande Armée.
Above, The Fraternity's monumental gate (Architect: Johann Otto von Spreckelsen). 35 stairs 110 m high, 106 m large, completing the great perspective from the Louvre and the Champs-Elysées.
Below: The Tomb of the Unknown Soldier.

Along the Champs-Elysées.

The Madeleine Church, an imitation of a Greek temple, was commissioned by Napoleon in 1806 to the glory of the French armies. It was consecrated in 1842.

The Place Vendôme, built between 1685 and 1720 by Boffrant and Hardouin-Mansart according to an octagonal layout conceived by Louvois. The 44 m (approx. 130 ft) column is topped by a statue of Napoleon and covered by an historiated bronze spiral, melted from the 1200 cannons seized at Austerlitz. ►

The Rue Royale, the Place de la Concorde, and the Palais Bourbon.

The flower market, Place de la Madeleine.

The Théâtre de l'Opéra (1861-1875), National
Academy of Music, designed by Charles Garnier in an
effort to create a style unique to the Second Empire.
It is one of the world's largest opera houses, with
11,000 m˝ of surface allocated essentially to the
stage, the artists and sets. As a result it only has a
capacity to seat 2200 spectators.

Opposite: The great staircase

Below: The principal façade facing the Place de l'Opéra. The dome
corresponds to the auditorium itself, with the pediment, topped by
Apollo with his lyre, marking the start of the stage roof.

The auditorium.

The ceiling paintings by Chagall.

The fountain below the small rotunda.

The orchestra pit and the grand curtain.

The great foyer.

The dance foyer.

The Place de l'Opéra, by night.

Below: The west side, the pavilion of honour, formerly the Emperor's pavilion.

FROM NOTRE-DAME
TO THE TROCADÉRO

In the Cité, under the watchful eye of Notre-Dame, stand two witnesses to the first palaces of the kings of France: the Conciergerie, the concierge being the officer in charge of administration at the royal palace; and the Sainte-Chapelle, the perfect expression of the spirituality of Gothic art. Crossing the small bridge, we arrive on the Left Bank, the site, since the 12th century, of the University, which set up there in the wake of Abélard, a renegade from the Ecole Notre-Dame. In the course of the centuries it transformed the abbeys and villages around it into separate quarters of Paris. This Left Bank, the setting of university life and often turbulent, has remained what it always was. From the Place Saint-Michel to Saint-Germain des Prés, whose 11th and 12th century church recalls the might and power of the Benedictine abbey, a phenomenal cultural centre up until the 17th century. This thirst for knowledge and intellectual activity has lived on in the cafés of the literati as well as the great écoles, the famous lycées, the modern heirs to the monastic and private schools of the 12th and 13th centuries. The mock-antique front of the Palais-Bourbon takes us from intellectual power to political power, which sometimes blend and sometimes meet; again, we encounter the age of Louis XIV, with the hospice and church intended for aged disabled soldiers: an admirable architectural composition best viewed from the Pont Alexandre III. The vista of the Champs-de-Mars provides us with a smooth transition from one of the most magnificent 18th century buildings, the Ecole Militaire, to modern times with the Eiffel Tower, the Palais de Chaillot, the Seine front and the Radio-France building.

Notre-Dame, the choir and nave, seen from the apsidal gallery.

Notre-Dame, the parvis (square) and the three portals

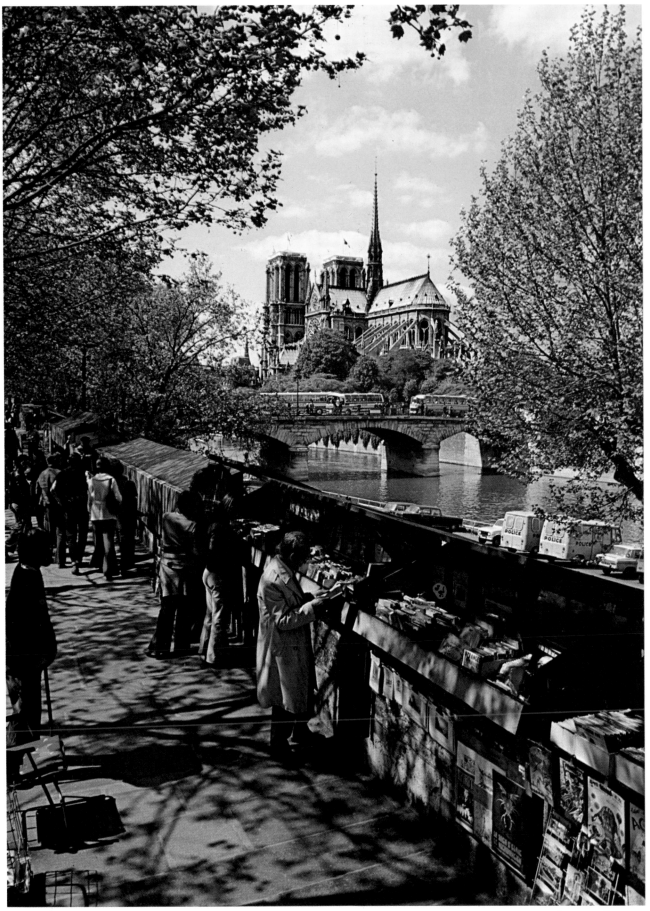

Notre-Dame, the chevet and south side, seen from the Quai de la Tournelle

The Palais de Justice (law courts), the first royal palace, was deserted by the kings of France after the uprisings instigated by Etienne Marcel in 1358. It later became the parliament palace, the supreme court of the monarchy.

The Sainte-Chapelle (13th century) built by Saint-Louis: interior of the high chapel.

Stained-glass windows of the books of Joshua and Ruth and Booz.

The Conciergerie, by day and by night: The Horloge, César, Argent and Bonbec towers.

L'Horloge, built in 1370, is the oldest clock in Paris. Sculptures by Germain Pilon (16th century) ornament the clock face.

The Place Saint-Michel: we cross the square
to reach the Latin Quarter, the oldest
quarter in Paris after the Cité. The square
itself is dominated by the massive fountain
built by Davioud in 1860. It portrays Saint-
Michel transfixing the dragon.

The Place Saint-André-des-Arts owes its
name to the church which used to stand on
the space occupied by the square before it
was demolished.

The Pont-Neuf, begun in 1578 by Androuet du Cerceau and completed in 1604, is the veteran among the bridges of Paris; above, from the Cité to the Left Bank;

opposite: from the Right Bank to the Cité - in the middle distance, the Conciergerie.

The Church of Saint-Germain-des-Prés, the most ancient church in the capital. It belonged to a might Benedictine abbey, founded in the 4th century. The oldest sections date back to the 11th and 12th centuries.

The Quai de l'Ile Saint-Louis; it was entirely divided into lots for development, and built up between 1627 to 1664.

The Pont de la Concorde (1787-1791), the work of Perronet, and the Palais Bourbon (1728-1807), the seat of the French National Assembly. The frontage, commissioned by Napoleon, reflects that of the Madeleine at the other extremity of the Concorde perspective.

Notre-Dame, seen from the Quai de Montebello.

The Seine at the Pont au Change.

The Church of the Dôme des Invalides. The architect Libéral Bruant had built the Church of Saint-Louis des Invalides, known as "The Soldiers' Church", as well as the buildings of the Invalides between 1671 and 1676. Louis XIV added the royal church by Jules Hardouin-Mansart. The work was completed in 1735 by Robert de Cotte.

Above: The Emperor's Tomb, designed by the architect Visconti, is an enormous sarcophagus made of red porphyry. The Count of Joinville supervised the translation of the coffin from St Helena to Paris. The obsequies took place on 15 December 1840, and the body was laid to rest in the Tomb on 3 April 1861.

Below: The garden in front of the façade.

The façade of the Ecole Militaire, built by Jacques-Ange Gabriel between 1751 and 1772.

The Invalides, seen from the Pont Alexandre III.

The Pont Alexandre III (1896-1900).

The palais de Chaillot (architects: Carlu, Boileau, Azéma).

The Pont d'Iéna, the Eiffel Tower, the Champs de Mars, the Ecole Militaire, seen from the terrace of the palais de Chaillot.

The Eiffel Tower machinery.

GUSTAVE EIFFEL

The Eiffel Tower, 300 m high,, was erected between 1887 and 1889 by the engineer
Gustave Eiffel. It is a unique masterpiece of equilibrium and lightness in spite of its weight of
7,000 metric tons.

The Seine and the Eiffel Tower, seen from the Avenue de New-York.

Scaled-down bronze replica of the New York original of the Statue of Liberty (a work by Bartholdi), the Pont de Grenelle, and the headquarters of Maison de Radio France (Henry Bernard, architect).

The Seine front, downstream from the Eiffel Tower.

The Pont d'Iéna, the gardens and the Palais de Chaillot. ▲ View of the Cité: the Quai aux Fleurs, the north side and the apse of Notre-Dame. ▼

FROM NOTRE-DAME
TO THE CHURCH ST MEDARD

After yet another rendez-vous at Notre-Dame, our walk will take us once again through the Latin Quarter, the student quarter of the Montagne Sainte-Geneviève. We will discover the Mouffetard Quarter and the three gardens situated in this area of the Left Bank: the Luxembourg, the Jardin des Plantes (Botanical Gardens), and the parc Montsouris.

The Church of Saint-Geneviève, started in 1758 according to plans by Soufflot, resulted from a vow made in 1744 by Louis XV, then seriously ill at Metz. The shell of the building was completed by Rondelet in 1788. Under the Revolution it was transformed into a pantheon, a secular temple dedicated to the Republican glories; it was again used as a church by Napoleon I, under the Restoration and Napoleon III. However, it later reverted to its Republican role under the Third Republic and became once again a secular necropolis; in 1835 it received the ashes of Victor Hugo.

The Rue Soufflot, the Panthéon, seen from the Place Edmond-Rostand.

The Sorbonne Church (Le Mercier 1635-1642).

The entrance to the Cluny Hospice (1485-1500) where the envoys from the powerful Cluny abbey in Burgundy resided during their stays in Paris.

Above left: the Avenue de l'Observatoire, the fountain by Davioud, the sculpture by Carpeaux representing "The four parts of the world".

The Luxembourg, a palace built for Marie de Médicis in 1615, was extended between 1836 and 1841, and now serves as the seat of the Senate.

The Gardens of Luxembourg: the Médicis fountain, under the shade of the plane trees (1624).

The Church of Saint-Sulpice was founded by the abbey of Saint-Germain-des-Prés; the present building was begun in 1646. The fine Italian style façade was awarded to Servandoni in 1732, and later revised during the 19th century. On the square, the fountain by Visconti (1844).

Above: The National Museum of Natural History and the Jardin des Plantes (Botanical Gardens). The statue of Lamarck, the evolution theorist.

Opposite: The parc de Montsouris (1868-1878), created by Hausmann: the Bardo, a reproduction of the Bey or Tunis' palace, presented by him as a gift after the Universal Exhibition of 1867.

The Church of Saint-Médard (15th-17th centuries) which was surrounded by the cemetery made famous between 1727 and 1732 by Jansenists abandoning themselves to convulsive demonstrations on the tomb of the deacon Paris. ◄

The Rue Mouffetard and its highly colourful market.

FROM NOTRE-DAME TO MONTMARTRE,
and the large parks of the Left Bank

On the Right Bank, at the level of Notre-Dame, the Hôtel-de-Ville dominates the square which in the past stretched as far as the Seine, to the so-called Grève or bank. Upstream, the Hôtel de Sens reminds us of the Parisian domain established in the Marais at the end of the 15th century by the Archbishop of Sens. One hundred years later, the Place des Vosges, built under Henri IV, set the tone for the individual hotels and fashionable apartment buildings constructed in the quarter by then conveniently cleaned up. These apartment buildings, restored and brought back to their true value in the course of the last few decades, recall the residential Paris of the 17th and 18th centuries. Other quarters of the old part of Paris, often insalubrious, have been witness to a new Paris, with the exception of a few period monuments: the St

Merri Quarter, the Plateau Beaubourg, the Halles, St Eustache, remnants of ancient parishes sheltered in the past by the ramparts built under Charles V; a wall, protected to the east by the Bastille Tower, of which only the square remains. The Place de la République corresponds to the site of the former Temple gate. More to the north, the Butte Montmartre with the Sacré-Coeur basilica, dominating the whole of Paris. We will finish with a grand tour of the large parks on the Right Bank: the Royal Forest de Vincennes, the Buttes Chaumont, to the east, and the parc Monceau, the Forest de Boulogne, to the west.

Notre-Dame: The rose windows on the west (12th century) and north (13th century) sides.

The Hôtel-de-Ville.

Above: the Place de la République was laid out by the Baron Haussmann in 1854 (monument and statue by Morice and by Dalou) at the site of the bastion of Temple Gate.

Right: the Place de la Bastille and the July column. The Bastille Saint-Antoine, built under Charles V, served to guard the Saint-Antoine Gate and the road to the east. Louis XIV having turned it into a state prison, it was stormed on 14 July 1789 as the major symbol of royal absolutism, and subsequently destroyed. The Column withholds a vault in which rest the insurgent Parisians killed in the riots of July 1830 and February 1848; it is topped by the Spirit of Liberty. Behind, the "Opéra de la Bastille" built by the architect Carlos OTT, 1989.

The Fontaine des Innocents. Under Napoleon III a square was laid out in the place of the church and cemetery of the Holy Innocents; it consisted of pits and galleries in which the dead were placed from the 12th century until 1786 when the tons of bones accumulated over the centuries were transferred to ancient quarries, the "catacombs"... The fountain, dating from 1550, was designed by Pierre Lescot and carved by Jean Goujon; it is located at the corner of the Rue Saint-Denis and Rue Aux Fers. A fourth side was sculpted by Augustin Pajou after it had been moved to its present site.

The Plateau Beaubourg: The Georges Pompidou National Art and Culture Centre (R.Rogers and R.Piano, architects), completed in 1977.

Bottom left: The Church of St Merri (1520-1612), erected in the flamboyant style typical of the 15th century.

Sculpture by Henri de Miller, Place R.Cassin.
The Church of St Eustache (16th-17th centuries).

The Forum des Halles, built on the site of the former central market halls.

The Saint-Martin Canal.

The Place des Vosges (1605-1612): the statue and the square Louis XIII.

The Hôtel Carnavalet, built in 1544, redesigned by Mansart in 1655. The Marquess of Sévigné resided there between 1677 and 1696. Its museum relates the history of Paris from Henri IV to 1900.

The Hôtel de Sens (1475-1507), the former residence of the archbishops of Sens, on which the bishopric of Paris depended until 1622.

The Palais Omnisports de Bercy, built between 1979 and 1983 by the architects Andrau, Para, Guvan, has the capacity to accommodate 17,000 spectators. With its internal modular structures, it can be used for all indoor sports and as a venue for large events.

MONTMARTRE: THE BASILICA AND THE SACRE-COEUR
The first stone was laid on 16 June 1875. Its consecration, scheduled initially for 1914, was postponed until 1919 because of the outbreak of the Great War I. (Architect: Abadie).

The bell of the Sacré-Coeur, Françoise-Marguerite, named the "Savoyarde" (16 tonnes).

View of the basilica from the steps of the square Wilette.

Notre-Dame de la Paix (Our Lady of Peace).

Le choir and the mosaic by Luc-Olivier Merson.

Artists, Place du Tertre.

◄

Montmartre: Place du Tertre; at the back the classic front of the Church of Saint Peter (12th century), the former abbey-church of the Ladies of Montmartre. In the background, the campanile and domes of the basilica.

The funicular railway, the basilica and the square Wilette.

Place du Tertre.

The Radet mill, one of the fifteen mills of Montmartre, also known as the Chapon mill, was moved to its present site in 1834.

Below: The apse of the Church of Saint Pierre (12th century). - Le cabaret "Lapin Agile", once a country inn, later, between 1905 and 1910, a favourite meeting place for artists and poets.
Rue de l'Abreuvoir: the pink house, painted by Utrillo.

The "Blute-fin" mill, also named "Moulin de la Galette". In the 19th century the miller converted his mill into a favourite crèperie for Parisians out for their stroll. Later it became a famous "guinguette", or open-air café and dance hall, as depicted by Renoir.

Anatole, the rural policeman of Montmartre and his kids known as "les Poulbot", named after the famous cartoonist, who portrayed the children of Montmartre.

The former Rue des Rosiers, today Rue "du Chevalier de la Barre".

Cemetery of Saint-Vincent: The grave of Maurice Utrillo and Lucie Valore.

The famous Moulin Rouge, whose shows, attractions, concerts and dances have been immortalized by the paintings, engravings and posters of Toulouse-Lautrec.

Above: His poster with "Valentin-le-désossé" and "La Goulue".

Below: The poster made for Aristide Bruant, the owner and club leader of the "Mirliton".

BAL
ROUGE
TABAC
Hamburger
TABAC
Hamburger
CAFÉ - TABAC
CAFE
TABAC

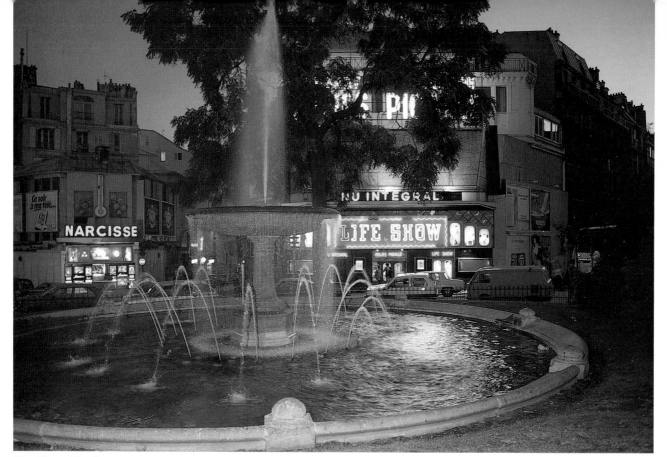

The Place Pigalle, once the quarter of painters and artists, today famous for its nightlife, cabarets and shows. At the centre, the fountain by the sculptor Pigalle.

The Place Blanche, its name reminiscent of the hill's gypsum quarries, and the "art nouveau" underground station entrance designed by Hector Guimard around 1900.

The Church of Our Lady of Lorette, dominated by the Sacré-Coeur of Montmartre. The church was built by Hippolyte Lebas between 1823 and 1896 and is modelled on the basilicas erected by the first Christians of Rome.

Place de Clichy: This was the site of the Clichy Barrier where the heroic troops under Marshal Moncey fought off the Russian troops for many hours on 30 March 1814. The event is commemorated by the central monument by Doublemard (1869).

Place Pigalle: Pigeons and daytime tranquillity.

In 1859 Napoleon III annexed eleven districts, several featuring gardens and private parks. Haussmann used them to create, among others, the parks of the Buttes Chaumont and Monceau; similarly, he laid out the forests of Vincennes and Boulogne, initially royal and later imperial estates donated by Napoleon III to the city of Paris.

Above: The lake and temple, the bridge and the footbridge of the Buttes-Chaumont.

Opposite: In the Forest de Boulogne, the Bagatelle park and the pavilion built by Bellanger in less than three months in 1775 for the Count of Artois.

Below: The Parc Monceau, which was landscaped in 1778 by Carmontelle for Philippe, Duc d'Orléans: The Naumachie.

The Forest of Vincennes: the Lac Daumesnil (12 hectares) and the small temple on the isle of Reuilly.

The Place de la Nation, formerly Place du Trône; at the centre of the roundabout the monumental "Triumph of the Republic" by Dalou (insert detail); further on, two columns top the toll houses of the Trône barrier, a work by Ledoux (1788).

The Parc des Princes sports stadium.

The mill of Longchamp, at the end of the racecourse.

The lake in the Forest of Boulogne. ▶

Orly Airport, 14 km from Notre-Dame, to the south of Paris.

The Concorde

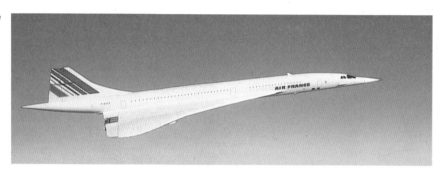

Roissy Airport, 27 km from Notre-Dame, to the north-east of Paris.

THE PALACE OF VERSAILLES

Driven by two main concerns, firstly to distance himself from the middle classes and the people of Paris, whose inclination for the Fronde and its uprisings had marked his childhood, and secondly to keep control over the lords if not the entire nobility, Louis XIV transformed the hunting home of Louis XIII to settle there with his government, creating a sumptuous royal city, a temple of absolute power, where etiquette and protocol ruled supreme over the proceedings at the court of the first of the world's monarchs.

In a park several leagues in length and breadth, the visitor is able to dialogue with a nature tamed to the scale of man by the genius of the gardener and landscaper Le Nôtre, and populated Olympia-like with deities respectful of classic mythology.

Away from the palace and its crowds, the kings sought the gentle peace and tranquillity of the Grand-Trianon, built for Louis XIV by Hardouin-Mansart. The Petit-Trianon, less stately perhaps, reflects the grace and elegance of the women who frequented it. The sensitivity prevalent at the close of the 18th century and the love of a less conditioned nature, a harbinger of Romanticism, are expressed in the alleys, the river, the lake and the graceful Temple of Love set in the landscape gardens.

It was here that Marie-Antoinette came to seek solace in a rustic setting, in a hamlet both pastoral, conventional and charming.

The ornamental pond and quadriga of Apollo, by Tuby; the Tapis Vert (Green Carpet), the round pool dedicated to Latona, the terrace and façade of the main body of the Palace.

The grand water display in the Latona pool.

"Queen Marie-Antoinette and her children",
after Madame Vigée Lebrun.

The reflecting pools, in front of the terrace
and the façade, bordered by bronze
figurines of the rivers and streams of the
kingdom: here, the Rhône.

Louis XIV, by Mignard.

The gate of the forecourt or Ministers' Courtyard.

The Orangerie, a work by Hardouin-Mansart.

The Grand-Trianon, built by Hardouin-Mansart, to allow Louis XIV to withdraw from the court.

Below: The gardens of the Petit-Trianon: the Queen's hamlet and house.

Statue of Louis XIV, in front of the entrance to the Royal Courtyard.

THE PALACE OF FONTAINEBLEAU

Around the keep of the old royal castle dating back to Louis VII, François I ordered the construction of a palace inspired by the princely homes of Italy yet fashioned "à la française". His intention was to create a model of the art of living, a masterpiece of humanist culture and ornamentation.

After the Valois, whose attention was diverted from construction work by the ordeals of the civil wars, Henri IV resumed the work, as did his son, Louis XIII. Louis XIV, Louis XV, and Louis XVI, enthusiasts of Fontainebleau and its hunting parties, stayed there regularly, adding wings, apartments, and continually reshaping and extending the complex. Napoleon I made this Palace of kings his own, and put much effort into its furnishings and furniture. Louis-Philippe and Napoleon III were more or less successful in their efforts to restore it, and their stays at Fontainebleau were frequent and numerous.

Aerial view from west to east: In the foreground the Cour du Cheval Blanc (White Horse Courtyard) or Cour des Adieux (Court of Farewells), reserved for the celebrations, tournaments and carrousels of the 16th century. It was in this courtyard that Napoleon bade farewell to France on his departure for the island of Elba.

Napoleon's farewell to the Imperial Guard in the Cour du Cheval Blanc at Fontainebleau on 20 April 1814, by Antoine Alphonse Montfort (1802-1884) after Horace Vernet (1789-1863) - Cliché Musées Nationaux.

The entrance to the Cour du Cheval Blanc.

The Horseshoe Stairway, built for Louis XIII by Jean Androuet du Cerceau.

The Tiber basin and the round pool; in the background, the buildings of the Cour des Offices, created by Henri IV.

The Diana Fountain (17th century).

The carp pond, the pavilion, reconstructed by Napoleon; in the background, the Cour de la Fontaine.

Napoleon's bedroom.

Top right: the Counsel Chambers, furnished by Louis XV.

Centre right: The Queen's Chambers, often remodelled, in particular for Anne of Austria, Marie Leczinksa, Marie-Antoinette.

Opposite: The Chambers of kings Louis XIII, Louis XIV, Louis XV, Louis XVI, transformed into the Throne Chamber by Napoleon I.

CHARTRES CATHEDRAL

The original church, from the 4th century, was built on a sacred Celtic site. The present cathedral, which succeeded three churches destroyed by war and fire, dates back to the 12th century. In spite of renewed fires its construction was pursued until 1260, the year of its consecration. Sections were added in the 15th and 16th centuries. Since the beginning of Christianity in Gaul, Notre-Dame de Chartres has continually attracted masses of pilgrims.

Opposite: The northern rose window. The stained-glass window, to the glory of the Virgin Mary, was donated around 1230 by Blanche of Castille and King Saint Louis, her son.

Below: View of the south side.

The southern rose window (13th century), illustrating the Apocalypse.

View of the floodlit frontage and north side.

The screen (around the chancel): Jesus baptised by John (16th century).
The Temptation of Christ. The Canaanitess asks for her daughter to be healed (2 groups by Thomas Boudin 1612).

Royal portal, tympanum of the central picture window: Christ at the Last Judgement (12th century).

The Cathedral seen from the banks of the River Eure -

Lancets of the south rose window (13th century).

King Solomon, detail from the lancets of the north rose window (13th century).

RAMBOUILLET

Bernier, a counsellor of Charles V, built the first castle acquired in 1384 by the d'Angennes family. François I, on a visit to Jacques d'Angennes, a captain of his guards, died there in 1547. In the 17th century, the castle flourished under the reputation of Madame d'Angennes, marquess of Rambouillet, the life and soul of the most famous literary salon of the time. A financier later purchased the land and created the gardens, which he gave to Louis XIV for the Count of Toulouse, born of la Montespan. Bought again by Louis XVI in 1783 to use as hunting grounds, the castle remained state property and serves as a residence for presidents of the Republic. Napoleon removed one wing, and the buildings were furnished and transformed with more or less good taste.

DREUX :
Chapelle Royale Saint-Louis

The earldom of Dreux had devolved upon the royal family since 1556. During the Revolution it belonged to the Duke of Penthièvre, grandson of Louis XIV and la Montespan. His munificent charity had made him so popular that nothing could be undertaken against him. His son-in-law, Philippe Egalité, a revolutionary, voted for the death of the king, his cousin. The son of Philippe Egalité, Louis-Philippe, reigned from 1830 to 1848, and transformed the chapel built by his mother on the hillock of the former castle of the earls of Dreux, into a mausoleum for the family d'Orléans.

SAINT-GERMAIN-EN-LAYE

The first keep was founded by Louis VI and complemented by his successors with an impressive fortification. Louis IX ordered the building there of a Sainte-Chapelle, which preceded by only a few years the one of the Cité. On the feudal ramparts, which are still discernible today, François I built a Renaissance castle, which was converted under Louis XIV and widely restored at the end of the 19th century.

PIERREFONDS

Louis d'Orléans, brother of Charles VI, commissioned Le Noir, king's architect, to rebuild the fortress of Pierrefonds. Made Regent of the kingdom due to the insanity of Charles, he was assassinated by his cousin Jean Sans Peur, Duke of Burgundy, in 1407.Acquired by the d'Estrées family at the end of the 16th century, the square was dismantled by Richelieu following the rebellion of François d'Estrées against Louis XIII.

Napoleon bought the ruins in 1813, and Napoléon III commissioned Viollet-le-Duc to restore and reconstruct the castle from 1857.

CHANTILLY

In 1450, the family of Montmorency acquired the fief by marriage. From 1528 on, the Grand Connétable orders the construction of the Great and Small Castles, of which the latter, built by the architect Bullant, still exists. The last Montmorency was decapitated in Toulouse in 1632 for raising arms against Louis XIII and the Cardinal. The estate falls to the Condé through his daughter. The Grand Condé plays host there to Louis XIV, his cousin, whom he entertains lavishly in the sumptuous gardens. During the Revolution the Great Castle is destroyed down to the ground floor. After the emigration the Prince de Condé and his son set about the reconstruction of the castle. On the latter's death, his grand-nephew and heir, the Duke d'Aumale, continues the work, between 1875 and 1881, in the Renaissance style.

COMPIEGNE

Like all the castles of the king of France, Compiègne is surrounded by a vast hunting forest. Until the 18th century, the royal residence was narrow and hardly comfortable. Louis XIV ordered the construction of new apartments facing the forest. Louis XV decided to design an entirely new palace and charged Jacques Gabriel - and later Jacques-Ange Gabriel - with the task of replacing the old buildings gradually to prevent any interruption in the household's stays at the castle. The building work started in 1751 and were halted almost immediately with the Seven Year War. And while Louis XVI resumed the work, the royal apartments did not become habitable until 1785... The palace reached its heyday under Napoleon III and Empress Eugénie, who was very much attached to the surrounding countryside at Compiègne.

Opposite: The Empress's Chambers.

The coach museum.

Below: The frontage facing the park.

Printed in CEE
Dépôt légal 2è trimestre 1994